Editorial Project Manager
Mara Ellen Guckian

Illustrator
Mark Mason

Cover Artists
Denise Bauer
Marilyn Goldberg

Editor In Chief
Ina Massler Levin, M.A.

Creative Director
Karen J. Goldfluss, M.S. Ed.

Art Production Manager
Kevin Barnes

Art Coordinator
Renée Christine Yates

Imaging
Nathan P. Rivera

Publisher
Mary D. Smith, M.S. Ed.

Grades K–1

AAB Pattern Review

Name:

Directions: Color the sea horses in an AAB pattern.

Author
Holly Burns

Teacher Created Resources, Inc.
6421 Industry Way
Westminster, CA 92683
www.teachercreated.com

ISBN: 978-1-4206-5983-2

© 2008 Teacher Created Resources, Inc.
Reprinted, 2010
Made in U.S.A.

Teacher Created Resources

Table of Contents

Introduction

There are patterning and sequencing opportunities everywhere! Understanding, identifying, and creating patterns and sequences helps students develop higher-level math skills. Reading, writing, and spelling also require pattern recognition and sequencing skills.

Patterns & Sequencing begins by introducing different types of patterns designed to enhance children's awareness of shapes, pictures, letters, numbers, and words. Wherever we look we can find patterns. There are patterns in nature, in fabrics, in floor tiles, and on different animals. Children can experience patterns visually by touching objects, and by listening to sounds around them. Children create patterns throughout the day. There are patterns in their art, their building constructions, their daily routines (hand washing, teeth brushing) and their household tasks (setting the table, folding laundry, etc.). Can you think of more examples?

Sequencing is an equally important concept explored in this workbook. Figuring out sequences is vital for solving problems in everyday situations as well as in school. Sequencing the events in a story (beginning, middle, and end), retracing steps to find a lost toy, or simply telling someone about an event involves sequencing skills. Children learn to follow directions in a sequence. Timelines are also forms of sequencing and are often used in social studies. In science, young children can sequence life cycles and steps used in experiments. *Patterns & Sequencing* includes a variety of activities to help children use sequencing skills effectively and to give them the tools needed to transfer these skills to everyday situations.

Keep in mind that the activities in this book progress from simple to more challenging. Don't worry if some of the activities stump children at first. Encourage children to work through the activities at a comfortable pace. Provide the support necessary for them to be successful. Have fun!

Identifying Patterns

As children are exposed to different types of patterns, it is important that they are aware of the number of repetitions that they encounter and that they are able to make connections between similarities and differences in patterns. To do this, a letter system is used. A pattern that repeats after every two subjects such as *red*, *blue*, *red*, *blue*, *red*, *blue* would be identified as an AB pattern. If this pattern were created using interlocking cubes, colored tiles, or blocks, each red cube would be labeled with an A while each blue cube would be labeled with a B. Children should be able to transfer this pattern each time they encounter two subjects that repeat sequentially. Therefore when children encounter a pattern of *yellow*, *green*, *yellow*, *green* or *circle*, *square*, *circle*, *square*, *circle*, *square*, they should be able to identify it as an AB pattern.

Other types of patterns that commonly occur are ABC, AABB, AAB, ABB, and ABCD patterns.

An ABC pattern occurs when three different subjects are repeated in sequential order. An example of this would be *red*, *white*, *blue*, *red*, *white*, *blue* or *star*, *heart*, *diamond*, *star*, *heart*, *diamond*.

An AABB pattern occurs when two subjects are repeated at least two times each. An example of this would be *pink*, *pink*, *purple*, *purple*, *pink*, *pink*, *purple*, *purple* or *triangle*, *triangle*, *diamond*, *diamond*, *triangle*, *triangle*, *diamond*, *diamond*.

An AAB pattern occurs when there are two subjects, but the first subject is doubled each time. An ABB pattern occurs when there are two subjects but the second subject is doubled each time. Last, an ABCD pattern occurs when four different subjects are repeated in sequential order. Of course, letters can be used to identify many different types of patterns and can become as advanced as you wish them to be. For this book we have chosen to use AB, ABC, AABB, AAB, ABB, and ABCD to help meet the educational standards for preschool to kindergarten-aged children.

Use manipulatives such as interlocking cubes, colored tiles, blocks, coins, silverware, marbles, or crayons whenever possible when practicing pattern identification to help children transfer what they have learned to real-life situations. Eventually, patterns will help children develop higher-level math skills, problem-solving skills, and literacy skills.

I See Patterns Book

Think about different types of patterns. Brainstorm some patterns you might see during the day—alternating tiles on the floor, stripes on a T-shirt or cat, etc. Then, create a book of patterns using the minibook pages as guides.

Materials

- I See Patterns minibook (pages 5–7)
- crayons or markers
- safety scissors

Directions

1. Cut out the pages to create a book about patterns.
2. Arrange the pages in order and staple them together on the left side.
3. On each page, color a pattern.
4. Share the completed book with others and talk about the patterns.

I See Patterns

By _____

I See Patterns Book *(cont.)*

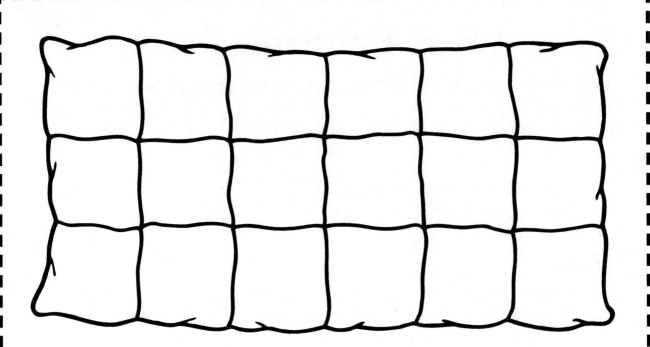

I see a pattern on the blanket.

①

I see patterns on the bee.

②

I See Patterns Book *(cont.)*

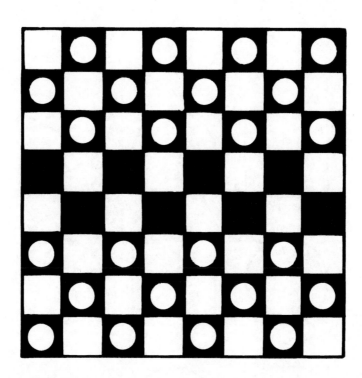

I see patterns on the checkerboard.

I see a pattern on the shirt. ④

Name _____

AB Shape Patterns

Directions: Draw the shape that comes next in each **AB** pattern below.

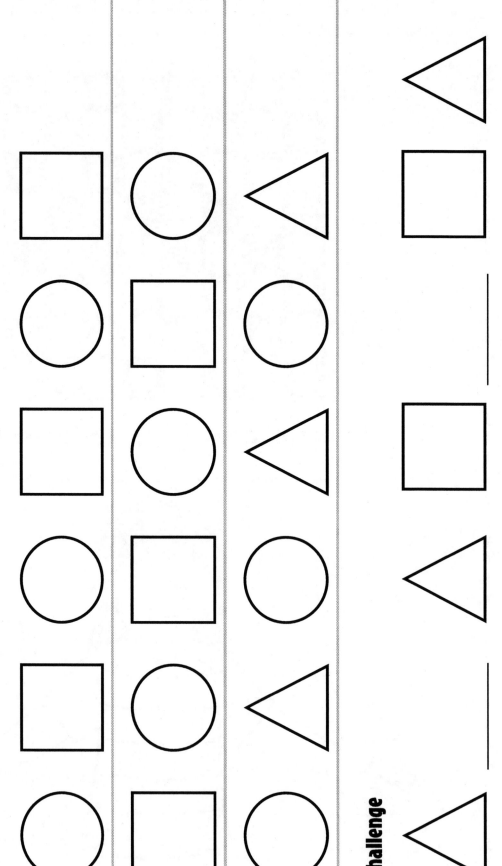

Challenge

Ice Cream Patterns

Name _____

Directions: Cut out and glue the correct ice cream cones in the **AB** patterns below.

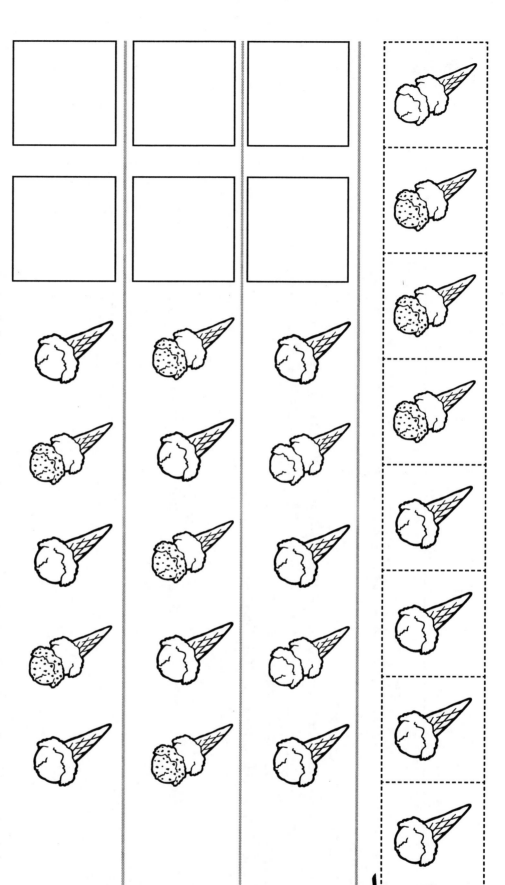

Name _____

Make Your Own AB Patterns

Directions:
1. Read each color word.
2. Color the boxes the correct color to make an **AB** pattern.
3. Use colored cubes, tiles, or blocks to make **AB** patterns for the other two rows.
4. Color the squares to match the patterns made.
5. Label each **AB** pattern in the blanks below the strip.

red	blue	red	blue	red	blue	red	blue	red
A	B	A	B	A	B	A	B	A

Name _____

Leafy Patterns

Directions:
1. Cut out the leaves at the bottom of the page.
2. Make an **AB** pattern with the leaves.
3. Glue the leaf pattern in the space provided.

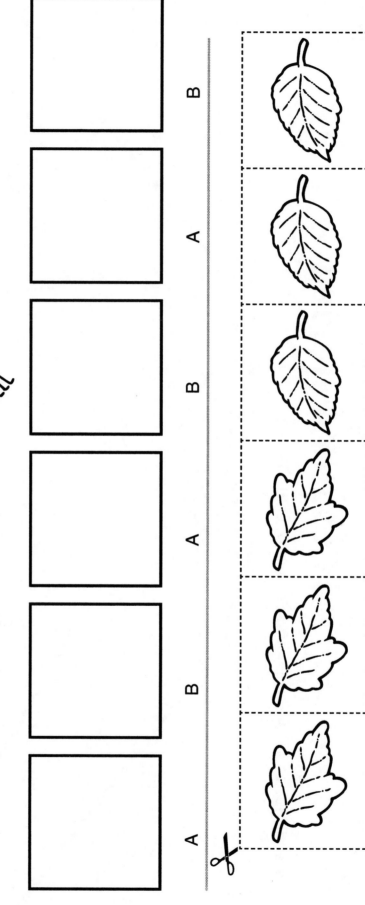

A	B	A	B	A	B

AB Pattern Review

Name _____

Directions: Draw and color an **AB** pattern on the T-shirt.

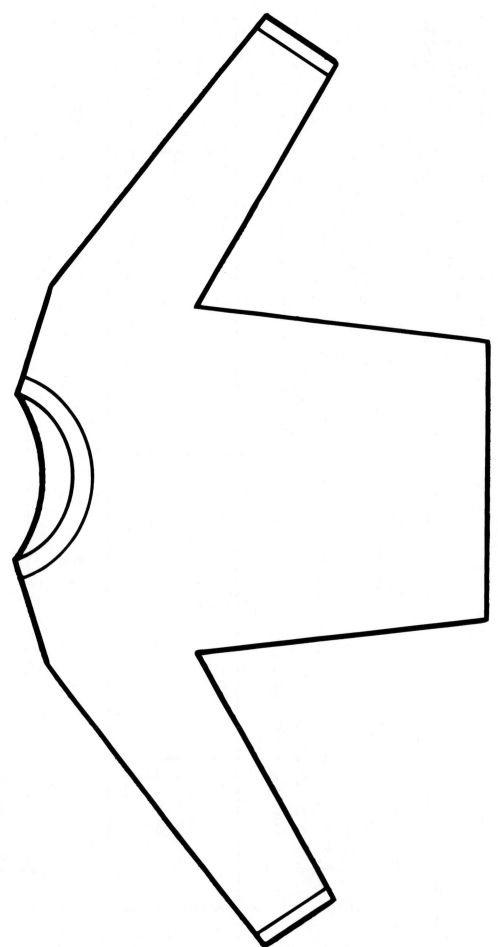

Name _____

ABC Shape Patterns

Directions: Draw the shape that comes next in each **ABC** pattern below.

Challenge

Name _____

Ladybug Patterns

Directions: Cut out and glue the ladybugs with the correct number of spots in the **ABC** patterns below.

Note: Extra pieces have been provided.

Make Your Own ABC Patterns

Directions

1. Read the color word in each box.
2. Color the boxes the correct colors to make the **ABC** pattern.
3. Use colored cubes, tiles, or blocks to make your own **ABC** pattern.
4. Color the squares to match your pattern.
5. Label your pattern in the blanks below the strip.

red	yellow	green	red	yellow	green	red	yellow	green
A	B	C	A	B	C	A	B	C

Name _____

Dinosaur Patterns

Directions: Cut out the dinosaurs. Glue them to the spaces provided to make an **ABC** pattern.

A	B	C	A	B	C

Note: Extra pieces have been provided.

Name _____

ABC Pattern Review

Directions: Draw and color an **ABC** pattern on the beach ball.

Name _____

AABB Shape Patterns

Directions: Draw the shape that comes next in each **AABB** pattern below.

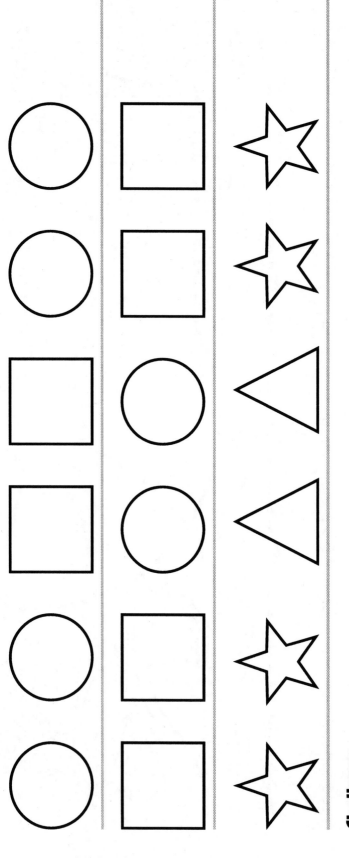

Challenge

Clown Patterns

Name _____

Directions: Cut out and glue the correct clowns in the **AABB** patterns below.

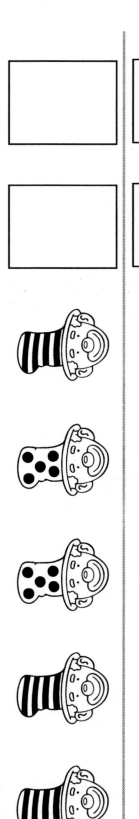

Make Your Own AABB Patterns

Directions

1. Read each color word.
2. Color the boxes the correct color to make an **AABB** pattern.
3. Use colored cubes, tiles, or blocks to make your own **AABB** patterns.
4. Color the squares to match the patterns you make.
5. Label each pattern in the blanks below the strip.

purple	purple	green	green	purple	purple	green	green
A	A	B	B	A	A	B	B

___	___	___	___	___	___	___	___

___	___	___	___	___	___	___	___

Name

Ocean Animal Patterns

Directions: Cut out the ocean animals. Use six ocean animals to make an **AABB** pattern.

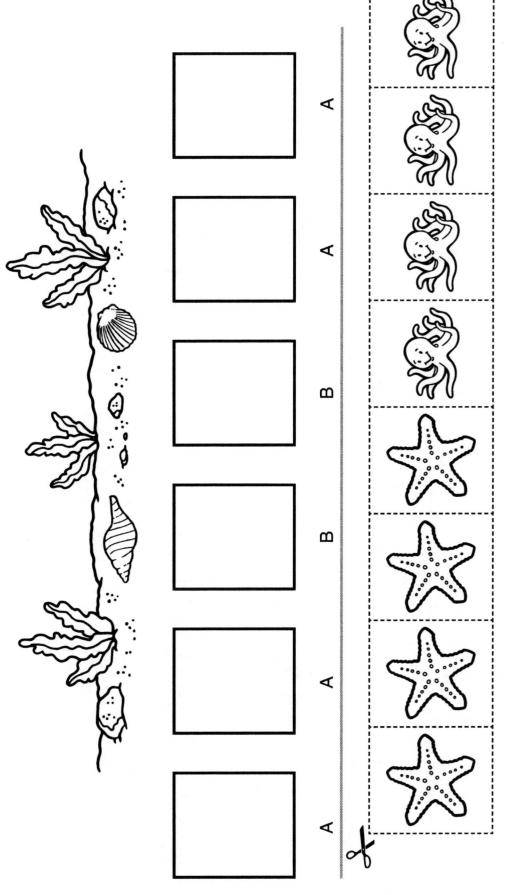

Name _____

AABB Pattern Review

Directions: Decorate and color the fingernails in an **AABB** pattern.

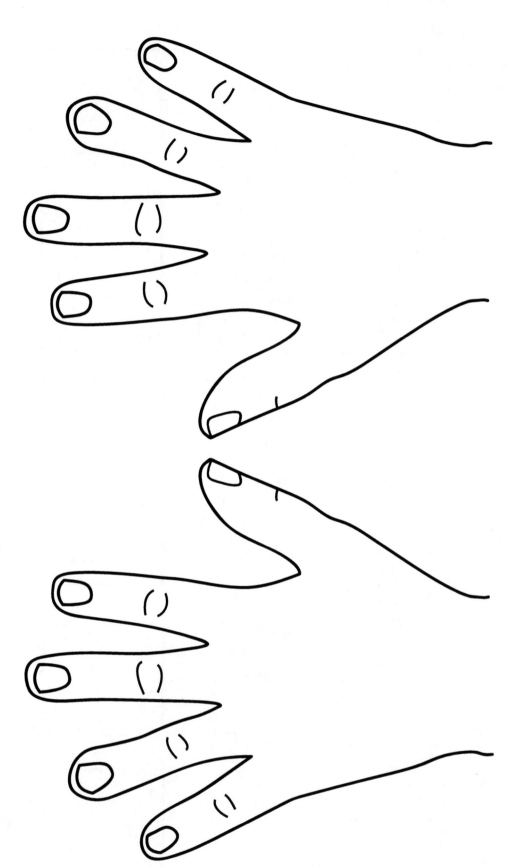

Name _____

AAB Shape Patterns

Directions: Draw the next two shapes in each **AAB** pattern below.

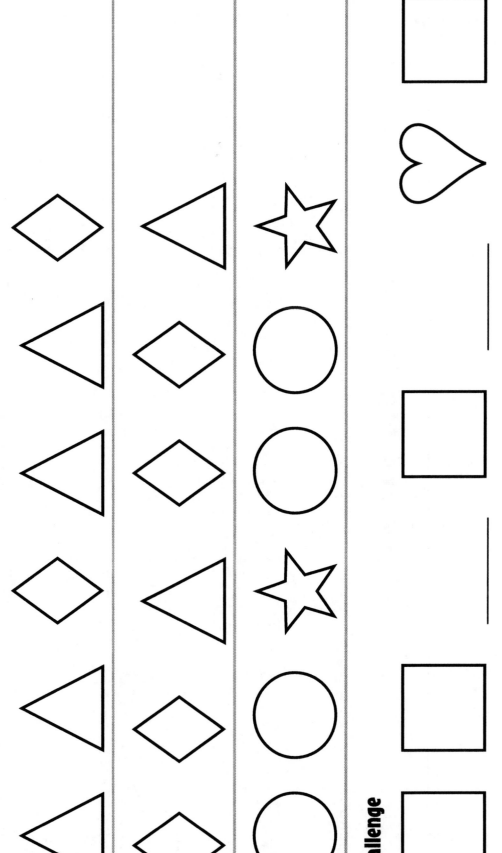

Challenge

Name _____

Sports Patterns

Directions: Cut out and glue the correct sports equipment in the **AAB** patterns below.

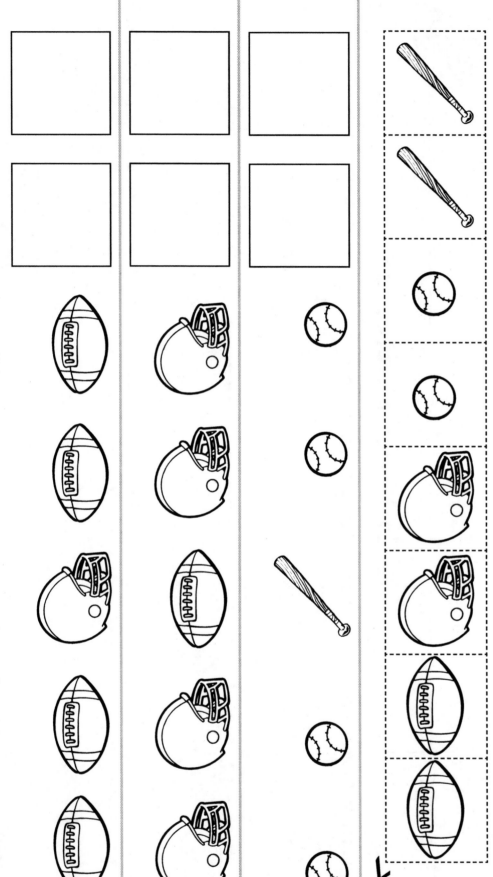

Name _____

Make Your Own AAB Patterns

Directions

1. Read each color word.
2. Color the boxes the correct color to make an **AAB** pattern.
3. Use colored cubes, tiles, or blocks to make your own **AAB** patterns.
4. Color the squares to match the patterns you make.
5. Label each pattern in the blanks below the strip.

orange	blue	orange	orange	blue	orange	orange	blue
A	B	A	A	B	A	A	B

_	_	_	_	_	_	_	_

_	_	_	_	_	_	_	_

Name _____

Snowflake Patterns

Directions: Cut out the snowflakes. Glue them to the spaces provided to make an **AAB** pattern.

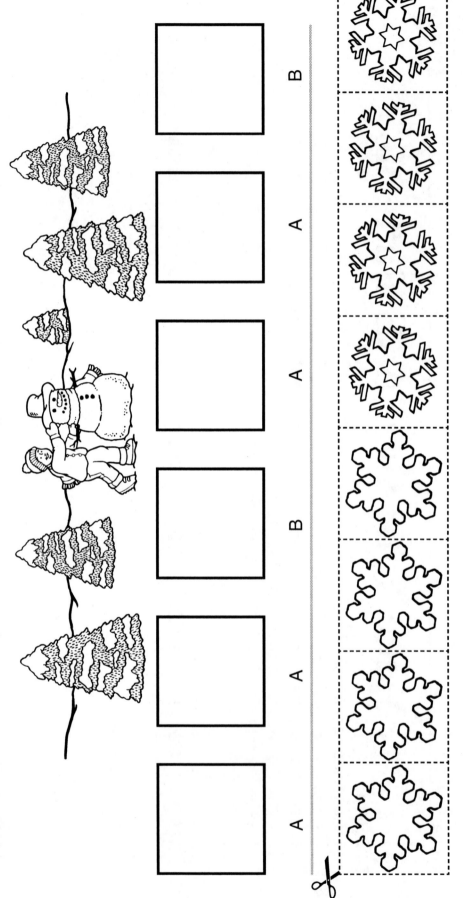

Note: Extra pieces have been provided.

Name _____

AAB Pattern Review

Directions: Color the seahorses in an **AAB** pattern.

Name _____

ABB Shape Patterns

Directions: Draw the shape that comes next in each **ABB** pattern below.

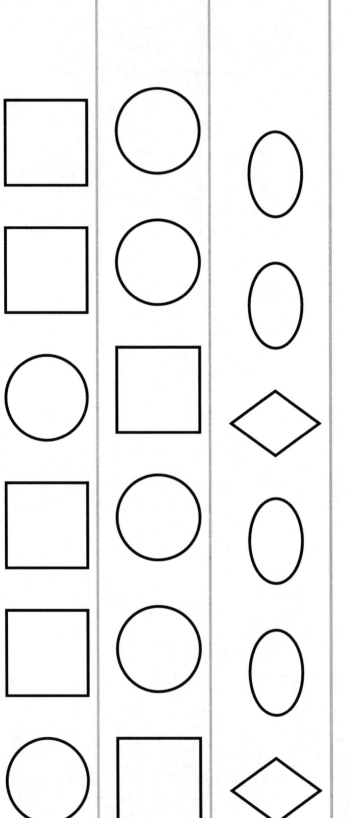

Challenge

_____

Flower Patterns

Directions: Cut out and glue the correct flowers in the **ABB** patterns below.

Note: Extra pieces have been provided.

Name _____

Make Your Own ABB Patterns

Directions

1. Read each color word.
2. Color the boxes the correct color to make an **ABB** pattern.
3. Use colored cubes, tiles, or blocks to make your own **ABB** patterns for the other two rows.
4. Color the squares to match the patterns you make.
5. Label each pattern in the blanks below the strip.

blue	yellow	yellow	blue	yellow	yellow	blue	yellow	yellow
A	B	B	A	B	B	A	B	B

_	_	_	_	_	_	_	_	_

_	_	_	_	_	_	_	_	_

Name _____

Food Patterns

Directions: Cut out the foods at the bottom of the page. Glue six of them in the spaces provided to make an **ABB** pattern.

A	B	B	A	B	B

ABB Pattern Review

Directions: Draw and color an **ABB** pattern on the quilt.

Name _____

ABCD Shape Patterns

Name _____

Directions: Draw the shape that comes next in each **ABCD** pattern below.

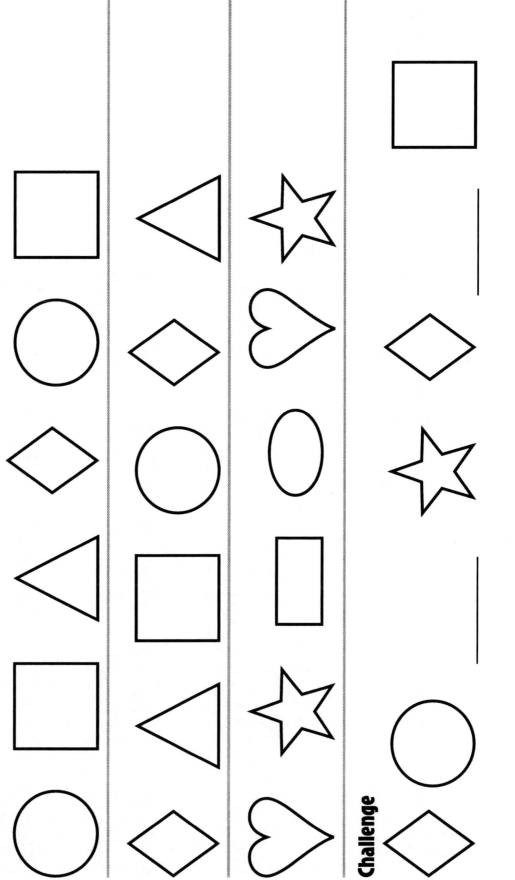

Challenge

Name _____

Present Patterns

Directions: Cut out and paste the correct presents in the **ABCD** patterns below.

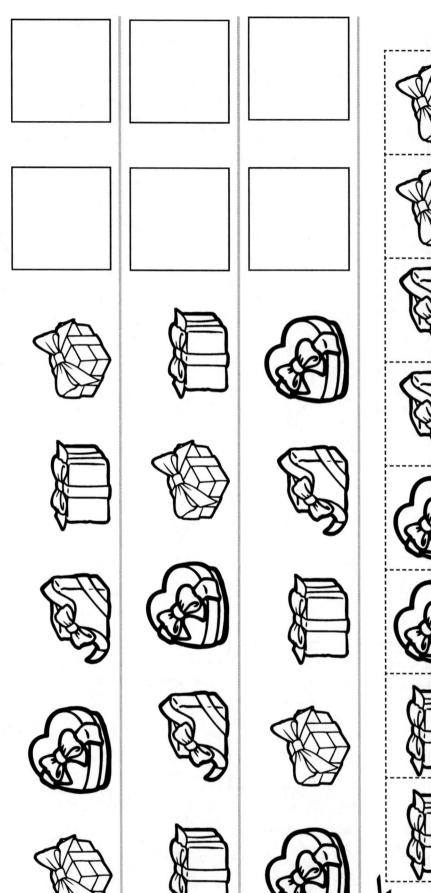

Name

Make Your Own ABCD Patterns

Directions

1. Read each color word.
2. Color the boxes the correct color to make an **ABCD** pattern.
3. Use colored cubes, tiles, or blocks to make your own **ABCD** patterns.
4. Color the squares to match the patterns you make.
5. Label each pattern in the blanks below the strip.

black	red	yellow	green	black	red	yellow	green
A	B	C	D	A	B	C	D

__	__	__	__	__	__	__	__

__	__	__	__	__	__	__	__

Name _____

Vehicle Patterns

Directions: Cut out the vehicles. Glue them to the spaces provided to make an **ABCD** pattern.

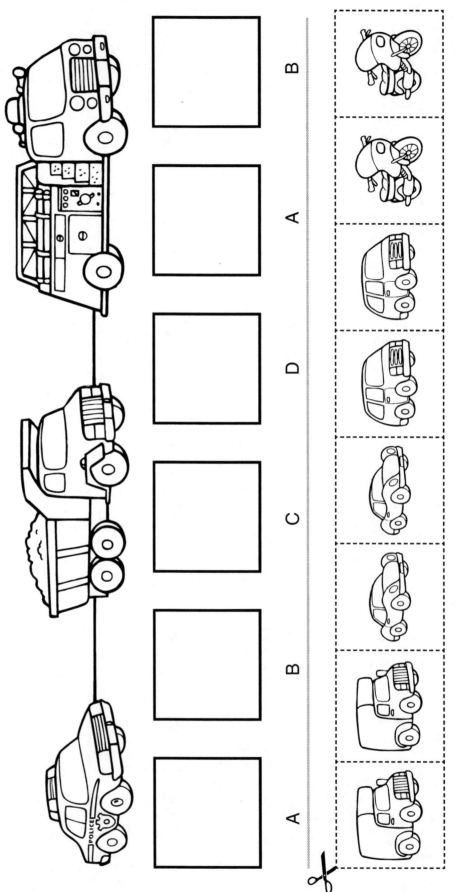

Note: Extra pieces have been provided.

Name _____

All Mixed Up

Directions: Look at each pattern below. Check to see if it is an **AB**, **ABC**, **AABB**, **AAB**, **ABB**, or **ABCD** pattern. Choose the object that comes next from the box with the diagonal line. Circle and color the correct picture.

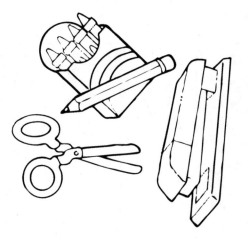

My Pattern Book

Directions

1. Cut out the minibook pages (38–41).

2. Put the pages in order and staple them together.

3. Draw, color, and label the pattern named on each page.

My Pattern Book

By _____

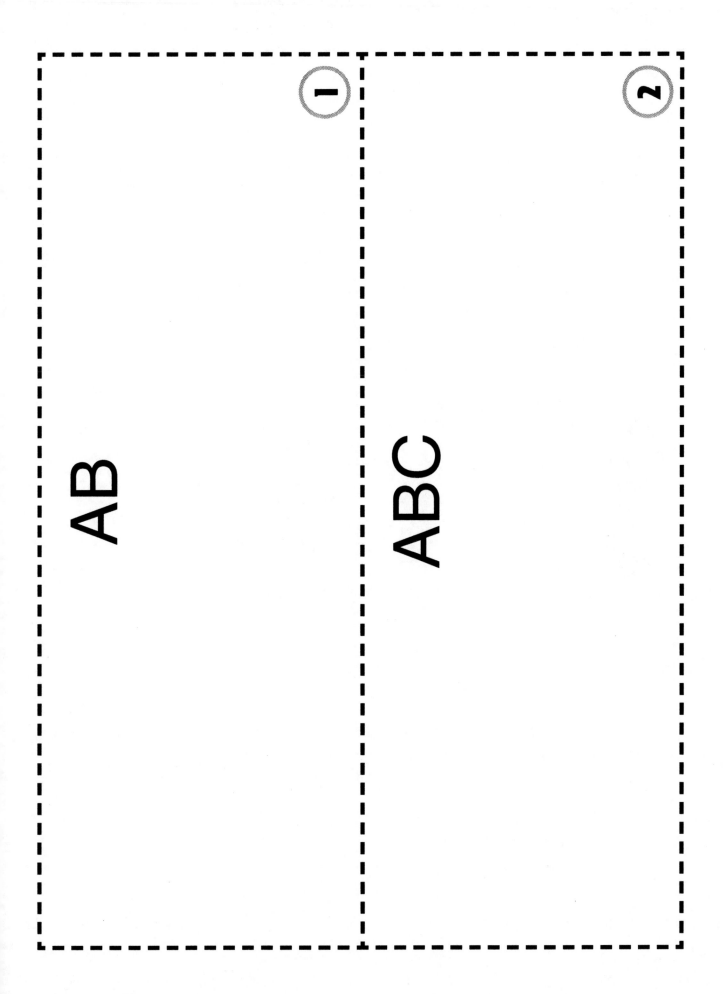

AB ①

ABC ②

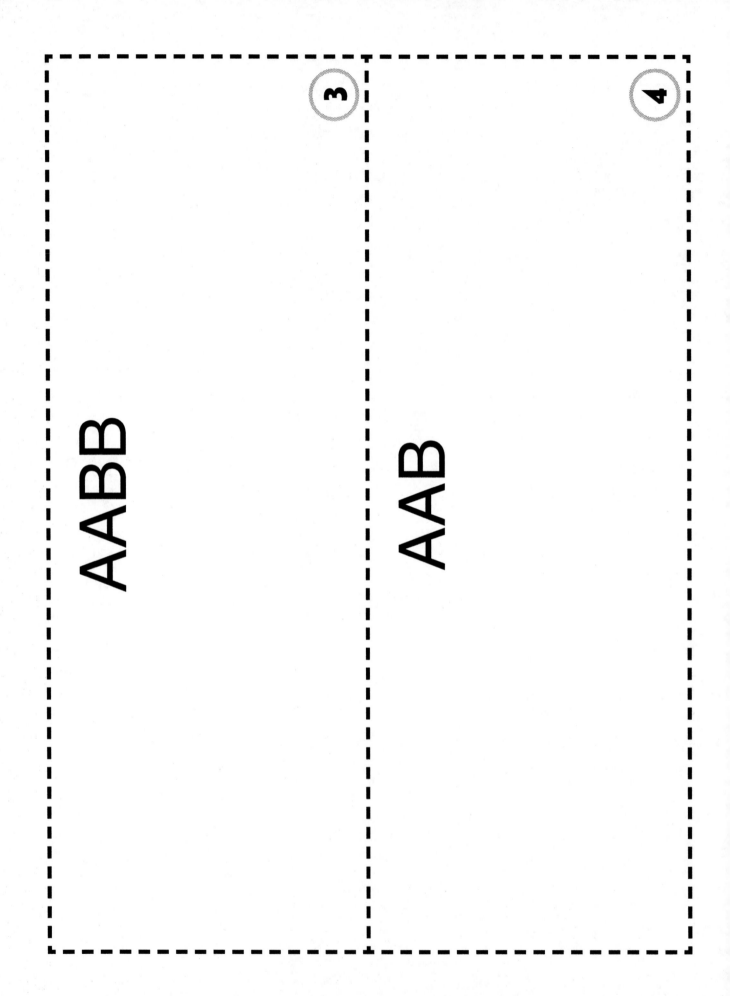

3

AABB

4

AAB

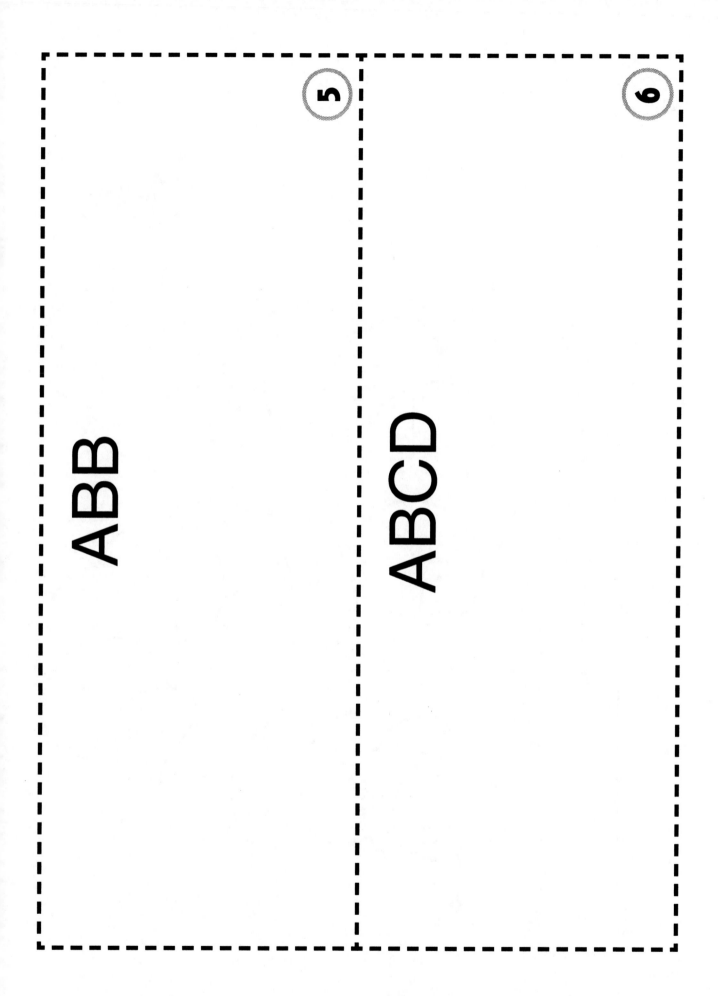

⑤ ABB

⑥ ABCD

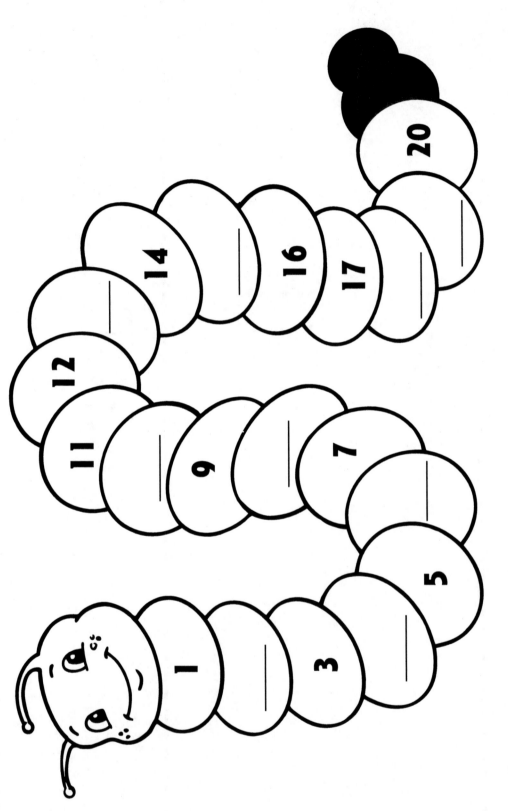

Name _____

Number Caterpillar

Directions: Fill in the blanks with the missing numbers.

Name _____

Counting Candles

Directions: Fill in the candles with the missing numbers.

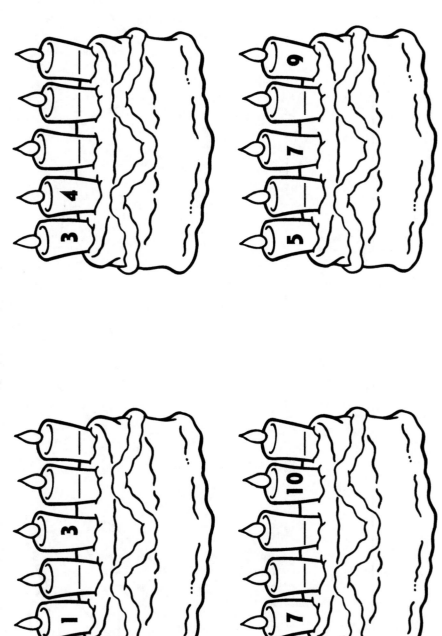

Name _____

Hot Dogs

Directions: Write the correct number on each hot dog to show the number that comes in the middle of the numbers on the hot dog buns.

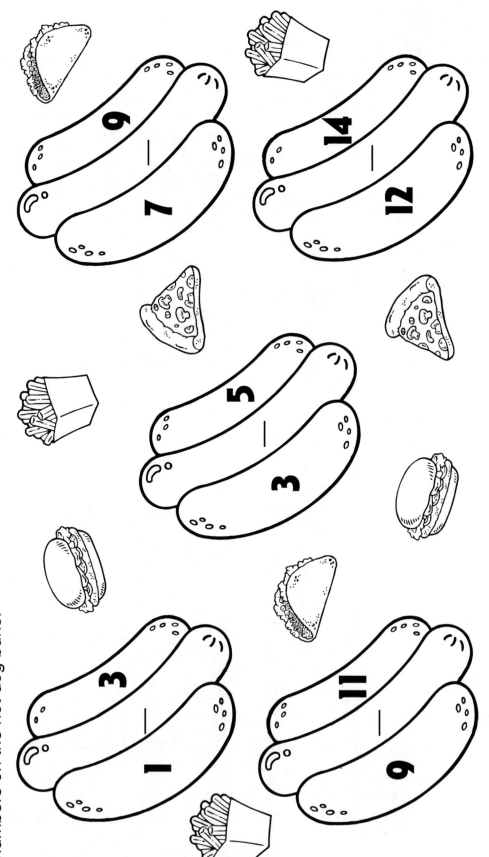

Before and After Numbers

Name _____

Directions: Write the numbers that come before and after the given number.

1. ____, **3**, ____

2. ____, **8**, ____

3. ____, **5**, ____

4. ____, **19**, ____

5. ____, **27**, ____

6. ____, **17**, ____

7. ____, **23**, ____

8. ____, **15**, ____

9. ____, **10**, ____

10. ____, **20**, ____

Name _____

More *Before* and *After* Numbers

Directions: Write the numbers that come before and after the given number.

1. _____, 4, _____

2. _____, 9, _____

3. _____, 6, _____

4. _____, 22, _____

5. _____, 28, _____

6. _____, 18, _____

7. _____, 24, _____

8. _____, 16, _____

9. _____, 11, _____

10. _____, 21, _____

Name _____

Number Dot-to-Dot

Directions: Connect the dots from 1–12 to finish the spider web.

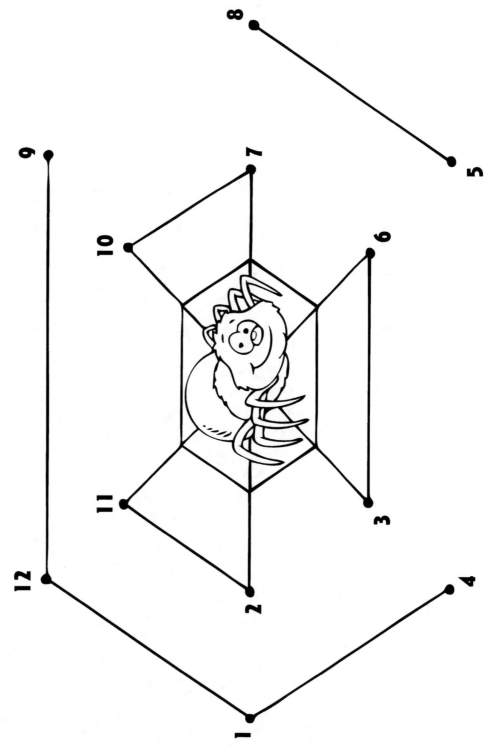

Name _____

Alphabet Snake

Directions: Fill in the blank spaces with the missing letters.

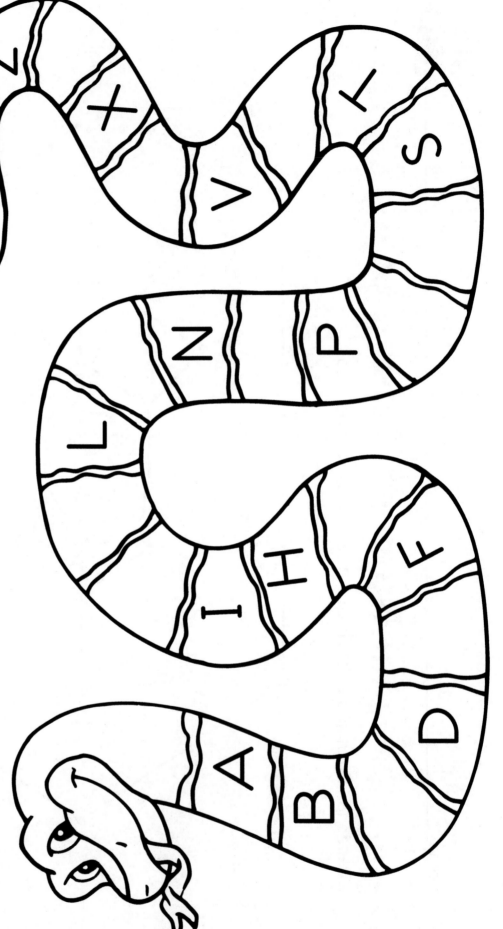

Time to Hatch

Name _____

Directions: Fill in the eggs in each nest with the missing letters.

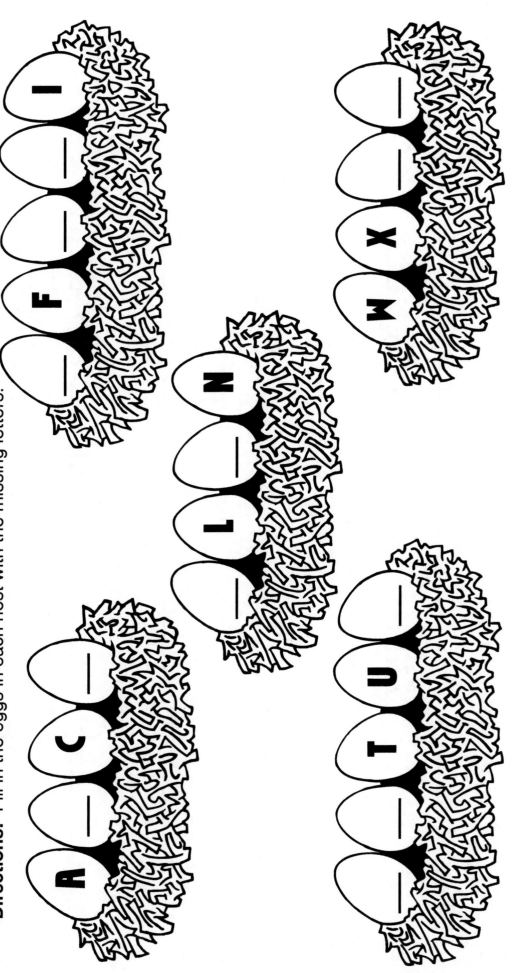

Before and After Letters

Name _____

Directions: Write the letters that come before and after the given letter.

1. ____, P, ____

2. ____, J, ____

3. ____, C, ____

4. ____, G, ____

5. ____, X, ____

6. ____, H, ____

7. ____, B, ____

8. ____, W, ____

9. ____, T, ____

10. ____, O, ____

Name _____

More *Before* and *After* Letters

Directions: Write the letters that come before and after the given letter.

1. ___, Q, ___	**6.** ___, I, ___
2. ___, K, ___	**7.** ___, E, ___
3. ___, D, ___	**8.** ___, L, ___
4. ___, F, ___	**9.** ___, S, ___
5. ___, Y, ___	**10.** ___, M, ___

Name _____

Butterflies

Directions: Write the correct letter on the body of each butterfly to show the letter that comes in between the letters on its wings.

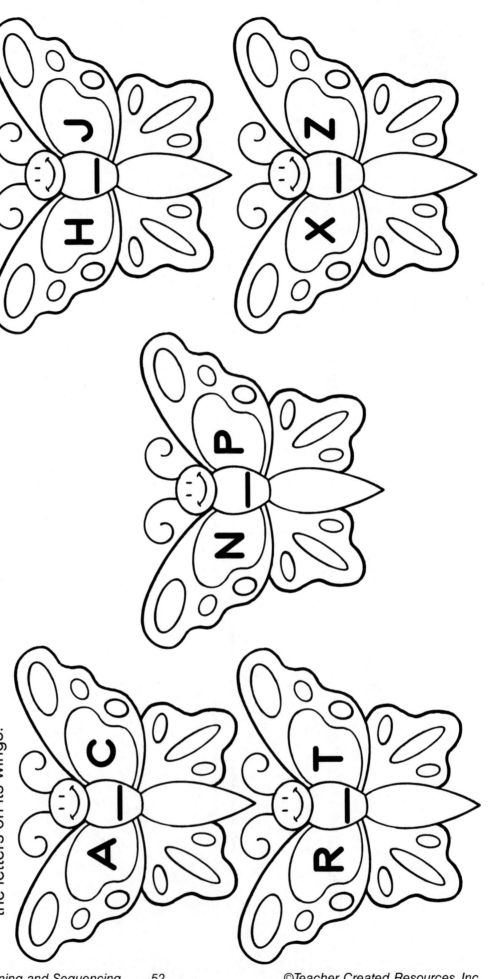

Name _____

Alphabet Dot-to-Dot

Directions: Connect the dots from A–Z to make a dinosaur.

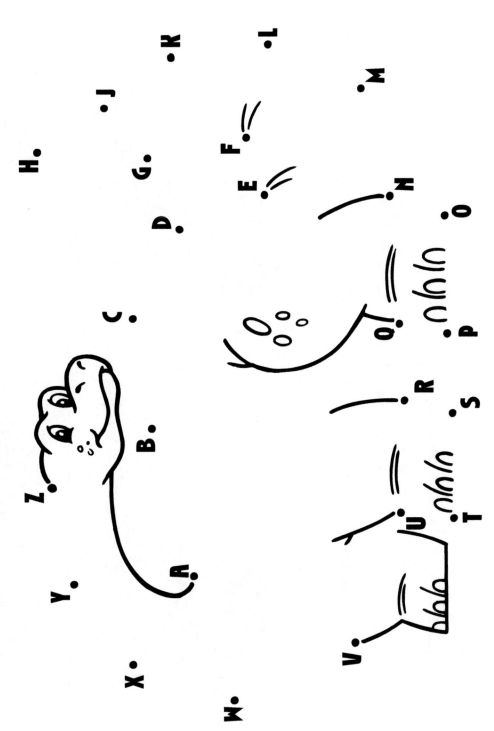

Name _____

Time for Cake!

Directions: Write the numbers 1, 2, 3, and 4 in the boxes to show the steps in making a birthday cake. Then, color the pictures.

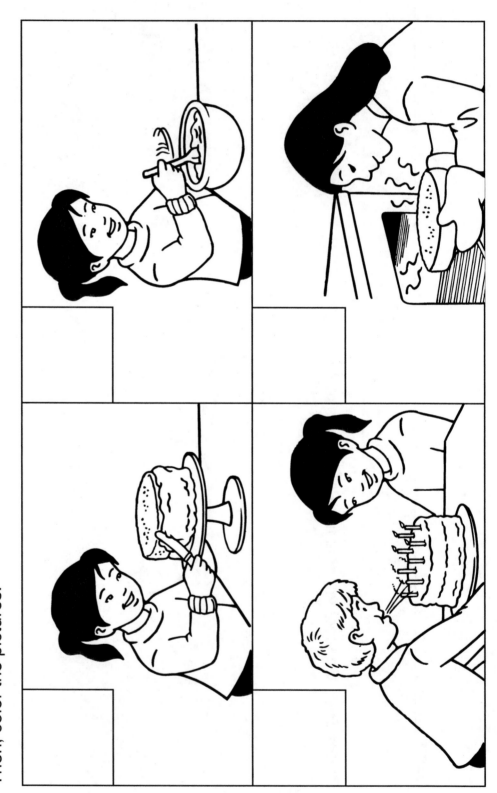

Name _____

Snowman Sequence

Directions: Color and cut out the pictures. Arrange them in order to show a snowman being built. Glue them in the boxes.

[ ]   [ ]   [ ]   [ ]

4th   3rd   2nd   1st

Name _____

Pumpkin Life Cycle

Directions: Cut out the pictures at the bottom of the page and glue them in the boxes to show the life cycle of a pumpkin. Color the pictures.

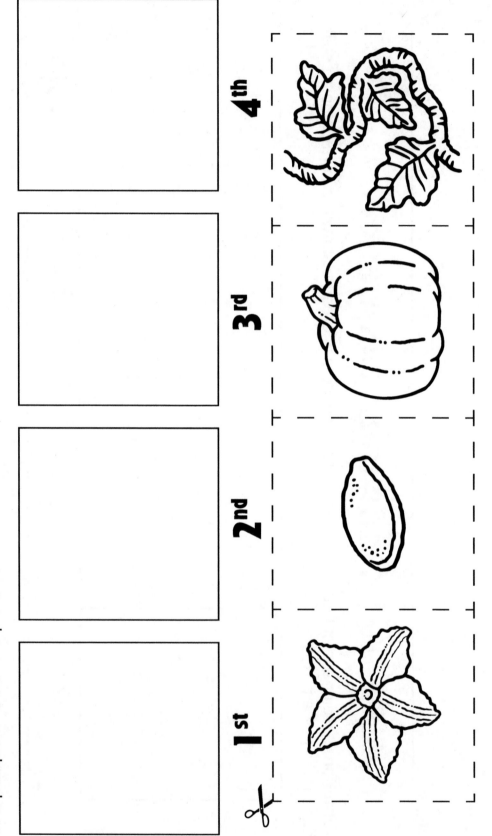

1st   2nd   3rd   4th

Sand Castle Story

Name _____

Directions: Color and cut out the pictures. Arrange them to show a sand castle being built. Staple the pictures together to make a book. Share the story.

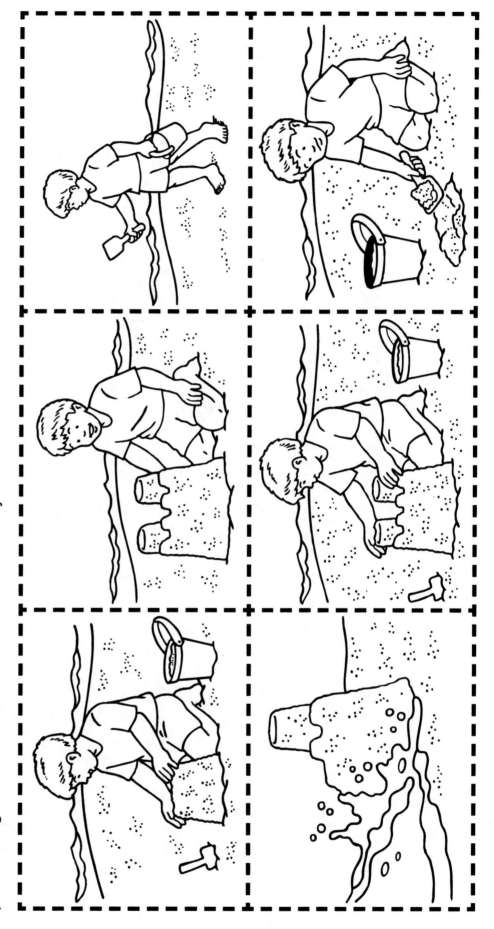

How to Make an Apple Pie

Directions: Color the pictures. Cut out the pictures and arrange them in order. Write the numbers 1, 2, 3, 4, 5, and 6 in the boxes. Glue the pictures in order on a strip of paper.

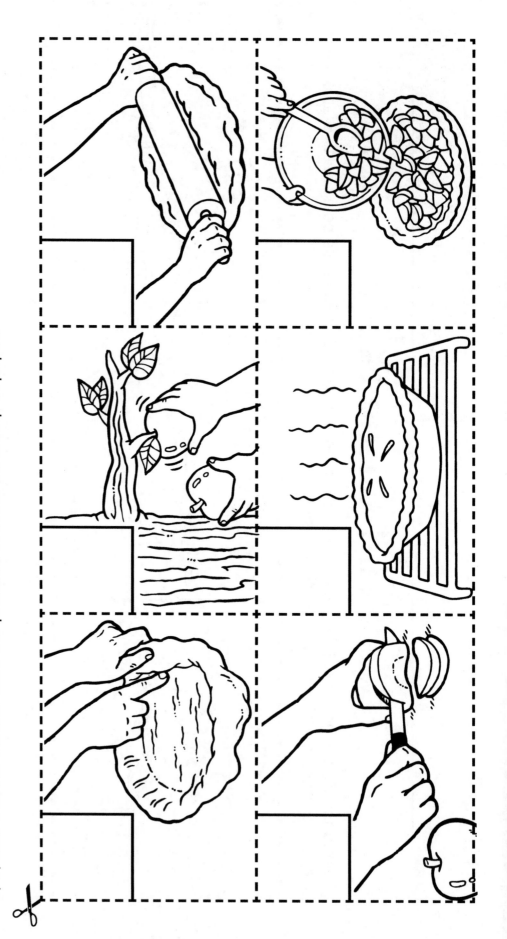

Sequencing Review

Directions: Put the pictures in each row in order by writing the numbers 1, 2, 3, and 4 on the lines provided.

Name _____

Answer Key

Page 8

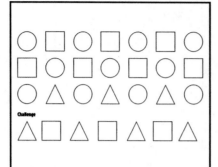

Page 9

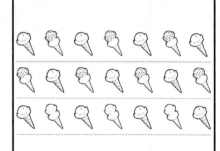

Page 10

Answers will vary.

Possible solution:

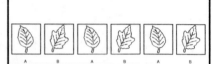

Page 11

Answers will vary.

Possible solution:

Page 12

Answers will vary.

Possible solution:

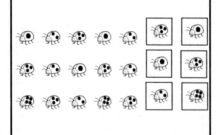

Page 13

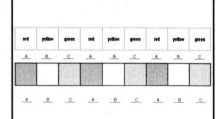

Page 14

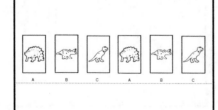

Page 15

Answers will vary.

Possible solution:

Page 16

Answers will vary.

Possible solution:

Page 17

Answers will vary.

Possible solution:

Answer Key *(cont.)*

Page 18

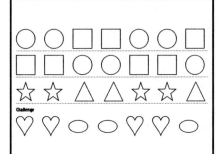

Page 19

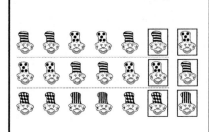

Page 20

Answers will vary.

Possible solution:

Page 21

Answers will vary.

Possible solution:

Page 22

Answers will vary.

Possible solution:

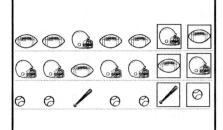

Page 23

Page 24

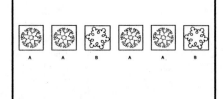

Page 25

Answers will vary.

Possible solution:

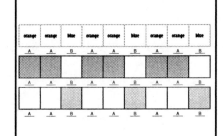

Page 26

Answers will vary.

Possible solution:

Page 27

Answers will vary.

Possible solution:

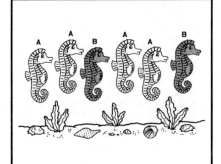

Answer Key (cont.)

Page 28

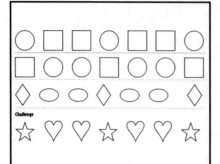

Page 29

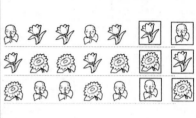

Page 30

Answers will vary.

Possible solution:

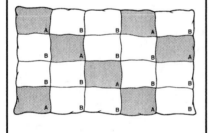

Page 31

Answers will vary.

Possible solution:

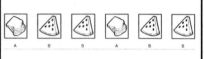

Page 32

Answers will vary.

Possible solution:

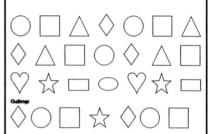

Page 33

Page 34

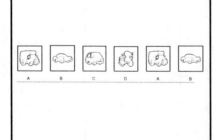

Page 35

Answers will vary.

Possible solution:

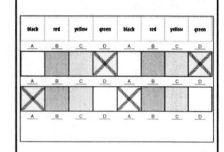

Page 36

Answers will vary.

Possible solution:

Page 37

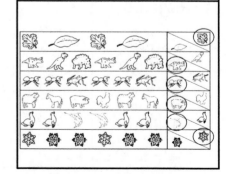

Answer Key (cont.)

Page 42

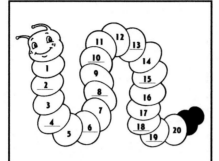

Page 43

Page 44

Page 45

1. 2, 3, 4	6. 16, 17, 18
2. 7, 8, 9	7. 22, 23, 24
3. 4, 5, 6	8. 14, 15, 16
4. 18, 19, 20	9. 9, 10, 11
5. 26, 27, 28	10. 19, 20, 21

Page 46

1. 3, 4, 5	6. 17, 18, 19
2. 8, 9, 10	7. 23, 24, 25
3. 5, 6, 7	8. 15, 16, 17
4. 21, 22, 23	9. 10, 11, 12
5. 27, 28, 29	10. 20, 21, 22

Page 47

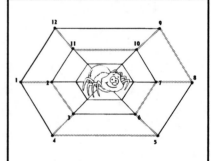

Page 48

Page 49

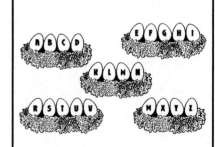

Page 50

1. O, P, Q	6. G, H, I
2. I, J, K	7. A, B, C
3. B, C, D	8. V, W, X
4. F, G, H	9. S, T, U
5. W, X, Y	10. N, O, P

Page 51

1. P, Q, R	6. H, I, J
2. J, K, L	7. D, E, F
3. C, D, E	8. K, L, M
4. E, F, G	9. R, S, T
5. X, Y, Z	10. L, M, N

Answer Key *(cont.)*

Page 52

Page 53

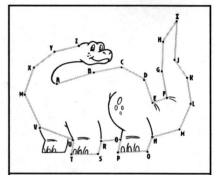

Page 54

Answers will vary.

Possible solution:

Page 55

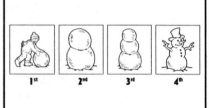

Page 56

Page 57

Answers will vary.

Possible solution:

Page 58

Answers will vary.

Possible solution:

Page 59

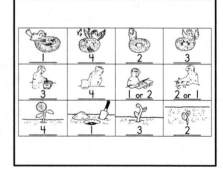